RHAPSODY OF SOUL

AN ANTHOLOGY OF POEMS

RAMESH CHANDRA PRADHANI

ISBN 979-888569039-3

Dedicated

to

the Almighty

whose grace

showers upon

me to ink some lines.

Contents

Contents

Contents

Contents

Contents

Preface

Beauty of a thing changes, life of a thing ages but soul remains beautiful and eternal . The melodious and mellifluous song of the soul enormously prints in the mind and heart of the listeners and the lovers of poetry. The realism and personal experience of the poet combined with the saddest and the sweetest feelings of the inside and outside objects of nature creates a rhapsody of soul . In the materialistic society people running after wealth need a little time to cheer the lonely and depressed mind to recover from the pensive mood. The present Anthology 'Rhapsody of Soul' is supposed to be the nourishment and so it will nurture the necessity of human beings in every walk of life.

Ramesh Chandra Pradhani

Acknowledgements

All the poems in this anthology are my original work. Most of them have already been published in various national and international Facebook Poetry Forums and some poems have been awarded with diploma and E-certificates, and also recognised with Poem of the Day, Poem of the Week and Poem of the Month.

1. HUDDLES MAKE US CROSS THE BAR

The world is full of plains and mountains

Life is amalgam of pleasure and pain

Luxury conspicuously makes us painful

Difficulties, adversity every life cheerful.

We build environment and environment makes us

No one can go against the law of nature in cosmos

Facing problems lead us to target solutions

We can ensure ourselves of every situation.

Life a race to face series of unexpected battles

Battles are nothing but sets of huddles

Which strengthens our capacity double

Inertia melts away letting everything flow

Whole body and mind flamboyant to glow

Huddles make us cross the bar if mollycoddled

Destination is no more far away to reach.

2. PLINTH OF THE WORLD

Clouds can never hide the sun
The old are gold not to abandon
The sky never falls us upon
Trustworthy not to shun.
Faithful who loves duty
Promised and committed
Derail not from the track
Born or made to be trusted
The brave are not losers
As gather courage from faith.
A ray of light shows the path
A flicker of hope to soothe
Faith the plinth of the world
Upon which stands the pillars
Of life to bear the load
Of roof to soak rains and sunlight
Fuel of life that moves on wheels
Technique to the clients to deal
Having faith makes us feel
All ailments of life it can heal.

3. STORM IN MY SOUL

Your red crimson lips
Waving inside my mind
Makes me mad to kiss
Heartbroken to miss
Glowing rose like cheeks
What my eyes strive to seek
Appears like gusty wind
In turmoil to weaken deep
Eyes with green eye doll
Fights with me to befall
Inside runs like waterfall
Bounces before me a ball
Little reddish nose allures
Enters to soul like an arrow
Creates a tornado to grow
Lavishly compels me to follow

4. HIDDEN EMOTIONS

Hidden emotions unless expressed
Turns to be a poison tree to be graced
Grows inside the core of heart
Without being able to come out.
Let the emotions flow outside massive
Share it to friends and relatives to gossip
Let the heart be fully relaxed
To allow something more to refresh
Suppress not the emotions excess
Save yourself from its oppression for recess
Hidden Emotions just like your own knife
Nobody can say at what time it may take life

5. IN YOUR ABSENCE

NO flowers bloom in the garden on my heart
No honey bees fluttering round
Deserted I am in your absence
Nobody there to understand my occurrence.
No pen ploughs the land of creativity any more
Seeds lying dead no more life to germinate
No soil can hide the grains underneath
In your absence still I have faith.
No lullaby muttered in the lips of a mother
When thou are in deep sleep for a long time
Readers feel worthless to chime
Even reluctant of turning over a page to see you further.

6. THE RESTLESS SOUL

Heart and mind separate but inseparable
Soul never silent when body uncomfortable
A little injury in body, mind can fast feel and react
Restless is soul in finding reason in fact
As life is a mixture of both cheers and tears
Story be comic or tragic the soul bound to hear
Soul the controller of each and every part of body
May obviously be restless in caring and guiding
Wants are unlimited to long for as per wish
Where mortals definitely deprived of divine bliss
Much desires of fulfillment drag away all humans
From their objectives of taking birth with no remains.

7. AURORA

Light bright mosaicness of refulgent sight
Creates madness in me to battle for the newness of far sight.
Conflation of diverse hues paints the word picture
To flow like a river of heartfelt emotions to capture.
Deep and dark colorfulness unfurls the complexity of life
The amalgam of diversities chimes in rhymes.
Each one has its own specialty, depth of purity
Mingling with others justifies the means purpose and entity.
Glossy picturesque on the canvas of the universe
Painting of lucidity and vivacity allure eyes lustrous.
Wonders of Nature always wondrous to perceive
Mesmerizes peculiar mind in hectic to conceive.
Let aurora comes in every life every day to have a new start
In quest of something unique to bestow upon the heirs to impart.

8. AGEING

Life is born and starts ageing day by day
Facing myriads challenges
Nobody can see how it moves each day
Emulating the huddles race to vanquish.
Time changes age, color and appearance
Stage by stage with a new countenance
Each step of life gets enriched with loss or gain
Some are gone but unforgotten, some forever remain.
Ageing of life is full of practical knowledge
Retains the best of things in storage
Tested and tasted by Time's circle
Once a helpless, but with aging does a miracle.
Time teaches a man and man a generation
Ageing process a source of inspiration
Telling the story of master mind
A warranty card leaving behind.

9. FRAGRANCE

Fragrance of flowers
Flood like showers
Honey bees whisper
Kissing the flowers.
Fragrance of love hidden
Felt by heart though undone
Mad are lovers human
Forget their domain.
Fragrance of wealth
Sweet for a while
Takes away smile
Characters defiled.
Fragrance of friendship
Bound in fellowship
Never found hardship
Till there is friendship.
Fragrance of forgiveness
Matter of great greatness
Changes worldwide ever
Magnanimity dwells there.

10. STOP SHRINKING YOU

The plant is planted beneath the soil to bloom
Tearing up the heart of gloom
Light peeps through the crevices
Similarly water downward rushes
Life destined to expand ahead
No matter what place and time made
One has to put his feet on the unknown
To make things confidently known
Football never rolls down unless hit
Stop shrinking before someone bit
Let things change to influence
The shape, size and standard
Possible only when you never retard.

11. CHOICE AND PASSION

Cheating a choice of one's karma
Anywhere anytime he can show a drama.
When choice is exclusively worst
Character is then and there cursed.
Loyalty not action but a passion for devotion
A sense of responsibility lifelong dedication
Loyalty can never be choosed by all
Unless and until intention is fair not foul.
Choice is not a passion but an action
Action without devotion purely pretention.
But passion reveals unconditional action
Action with nobility and authorization.

12. INNOCENCE

Moments of full freedom
Nothing can curtail
Dearth of wisdom
Tells many a tale.
Realm of purity
Nobody can spoil
Replete with beauty
Seeds of the soil.
No place of deception
No malice and conspiracy
Mind in concentration
Receives with accuracy.
A candle like shines at night
In place of the sun
Attraction of dim light
Lacking superstition.
Outsourcing joy and delight
Someone's apple eye
Same the inside and outside
Spreads like limitless sky

13. FRIENDSHIP

Understanding each other feelings and emotions
No matters are they in any situations
Unbidden caring one another in massive famine
Unsolicited presence in marriage or demise
Sharing pain and pleasure without expectations
Unconditional love with lifelong dedications
Inextricable togetherness in spite of motley fighting over and again
Like two mollycoddled dogs in inbred affection
Impetuous liking and feeling the importance of other
Undoubtedly brings the duo closer together
Impulsively paying respect to both likes and dislikes
Vehemently makes them complements alike.

14. MY MOTHER MY POWER

Speaking shadow in my loneliness
My mother my voice in silence
My mother my ladder to rise up
My hope in disappointment not to give up
Image of strength stands in my helplessness
Picks me up from the dungeon of selfishness
An unfurling umbrella in rains, sun and coldness
A furnace of warmth in my slackness.
My mother my rainbow in my clouds
A remover to wash away all my doubts.
My mother my power, my rapture
Enriched with protein and nutrition to nurture
It is only mother who can drink poison of all sorrows
To see her children living better for tomorrow
Make your life Poetic
Life is replete with similes and metaphors
Melody, music, magic regularly prosper to decipher
Mellifluous are the voices, sound and word pictures confer
Effulgent hues twisted in its mixture and texture offer
Language of expression, worldwide communication
Makes one laugh and cry with overflow of emotions
Rhymes and rhythm profusely evolves to chant rejuvenation
Hallucinations fails to erect the citadel of self realization
Life is a poetry recite it for your gratification

Read by heart, can heal the wound of tension

Dive into the heart of poetry it can move you the whole universe

However unknown, unseen and untrodden or far away

15. SUCCESS

Not the result of luxury and comfort
Sum total of small, smaller or the smallest efforts
Fruits of hard labour and incessant sweat
Series of many a failures and attempts
Daring steps to dream for the world community
Without being a dare devil to ruin the society
Courage to face any sort of adversity
Harvesting the crops of fertility
Accumulation of time, sleepless nights
Tolerance of physical pain to smile
Staunch belief in oneself and in action
Access to the domain of unknown association
Worshipping the duty with love and devotion
Erects the charminar of gratification
Self sacrifice to the honour of education
Liberates the soul of triumph towards manifestation.

16. MY LONELINESS

Depression not reason of my silence
Nor any weakness to finance
Nor retirement from life's business
My strength my loneliness
Shows me light to see the truth
Obviously the ultimate fearlessness.
No deception, no pretension
In my loneliness of extension
No reluctance, nor any distance
Just to bridge the generation gaps
May be platform to avoid the mishaps
May be the world to reshape
Commitment to do the wonders
Know not how you ponder
But I am sure to surrender
Me to the mighty mender
To forgive this offender
And beg His apology to render
Something extraordinary
Something miraculous
To unlock the doors of secrecy
With assurance and accuracy.
My loneliness my secrets, no isolations no regrets
Loneliness makes my fate, keeps me away from hatred

17. GREED

Greed is human, magnanimity divine
Nothing, in the mundane world, yours or mine
Greed makes one hanker after money to ease
He or she soars in the firmament of mirage
No blood relations cherished before the men of greed
Who themselves torture being niggard, no time to heed
Foul means their option to amass unwarranted wealth
Unfortunately the lion's share costs for check up health
Greed whacks the humble on conscience recklessly
Plays games of masquerades on simplicity whimsically
Intoxication of wan hopes burns the desires of dreams
Life floats on the bubbles of stream
Sojourning in the hamlet made of wax and straw
Knows not how uncertain his future, still obstinate to draw
The greedy make their own sepulcher to bury
By the summon of demise letting someone be merry

18. SONGS OF NATURE

Songs of nature
Unending rapture
Poet's mind capture
Nurture to culture.
Songs of nature heal
Wounds we can feel
Cure with eternity
Offering creativity.
Songs of nature magical
Melodious and musical
Make many a men moral
Immortalize being mortal.
Songs of nature alluring
Full of nectar and beauty
Tranquility so appealing
Novel gift of Almighty.
Songs of nature never ends
One after the other leads
The gap never found
To take everybody's heed.
A moment in her lap
Viewer's mind ever saved
Stay as lively as heavenly spirit
As long as the world exists.

19. LIFE

A four lettered word is life
Unfathomable is its vibe
Life is too small and small
But every small more beautiful
Who says life is temporary
That can makes history
Life is not only a short story
An autobiography, a biography
A drama both tragic and comic
Having diverse roles characteristic.
A novel narrative and descriptive
Speaks of ages since primitives
A song aesthetic and erotic
Without which man is a lunatic
A criticism analytical and logical
Reasons based critical, philosophical
A performing art always ecstatic
Makes one laugh and cry
A dance having NAVRASAS
WITH sixty four mudras
Hearts leap up when watches
Life is beautiful, life is valuable
Life is a chance be mindful.
Be grateful to God to make fruitful.

20. BLISS OF LONELINESS

A blessing in disguise in my world of creativity

Let me whelve under the canopy of serenity

Where I discern the presence of Almighty

In His creation camouflaged the inner veracity .

An wireless connective to join with the Unseen

Vigorous means of communication so soothing

A podium before the worldwide audience

To expose myself to pass the universal message of His essence.

A moment of unbridled enthusiasm to express

Persuasive speech of humanity in the language of silence

Delved into the realm of reverberating reformation

Always in quest of love, peace, harmony and unification.

Reticence in loneliness speaks something uncommon

Divine graces of blessedness showers upon

The large hearts of mankind, the men of letters

Present the society a priceless gift that vehemently flatters.

21. ENVIRONMENT DAY

Environment is man made in his own will

Bear whether good or bad up to his own deal

Make a neat and clean shade to refill

The grass to grace, the green to bless not a task uphill

Let the tree of humanity be planted

All the roots of social problems be uprooted

Be the worshipper of nature to nurture

Erase the scars of negativity from mind immature

Each day five minutes enough to to devote

For better world of peace and love to innovate

Just some physical pain for pleasure to allocate

Man's selfishness be smashed for novelty to obsolete

Keep the environment dirt less to keep you fine

Enrich the environment with greenness to be rich in time

Decorate the environment with freshness to shine

Let the environment writes the songs of joy to chime

Dream not to cut the branch you sit on for rest

Thou are the cause and effect of consequences

Take time to introspect the works done in haste

Do in time to recover the loss already endured in sequences.

22. GIRLS DAY OUT IN PARIS

A day out in Paris
Carries memories
Of life freedom
Nice kingdom.
Life is joyful when
Friends join hands
Time passes away
Worries far away.
Freed girls choices
Always embrace
Touring out a day
Makes them gay.
Emotions shared
Hearts get lighted
Tensions forgotten
From top to bottom.
Lovely gift of God
Life be short cut
Fill the purpose
Life will be just.

23. RECONCILATION

Restoration of present with past gives birth to revolt and revival
Fetches rejuvenation and reverberation for life's survival
Neither the past nor the present can individually shape the fate of future
As the amalgam of seasons does nurture the Nature.
Unless and until intermingled are pain and pleasure
No life can breathe in and out, pulse to measure
The old are to depart the stage but not before without leaving something essential
For the new comers to fill the gap with non academic credentials
Footprints left often rectifies the weakness of the Present
Reunion of lost love as if regained paradise
Juxtaposed each other to plough the land of love and peace
Sow the seeds of gail and gaiety to avoid malice
Dreaming to pluck the fruits of eternal bliss
To share the same to the mankind with god's grace
A placating promise to rebuild the devastated fort
Surrounded by the walls of resolution to escort
The second chance of mending the best of the nest
To hatch the eggs of humanity to come out
The golden siblings of future to safeguard unhurt.

24. AMBITION

A long distance to cover within the track simply ambition
Without being collided with anything or anybody leaving the junction
Paves the way to highway for smooth and comfort journey
Nothing can detract the traveler from the path of honey.
Ambition born with the birth of a life to move
But Time does not let all on the same way
Some lose it swaying in the swing of luxury
Men of actions aim at the target to prove
Let not life be the aimless vagabond to ruin
Hold the mirror of ambition to dress, race to win
Where there's life, there's destination to reach
The road taken makes the difference to teach
Life without ambition meaningless to His miraculous creation
Purpose unserved as if forsaken an accursed habitation
Reverberation of life decelerates the glow of its rejuvenation
Locked down even the normal activities and transportation.

25. EVERYONE TEACHES A LESSON

Hate not a beggar having nothingness
He teaches how to stay in happiness
Love not the rich having everything
Poor are they in mind and heart to give anything
Detest not the poor having nothing to offer others
Who grant us opportunity, wealth to gather?
Blame not the bad people not bad from birth
Feel proud of them who show us right path with mirth .
Revenge not upon the enemies who are often true friends
Welcome them cordially who never allow us to do the wrong
Keep in mind everyone teaches us a lesson
No matters in what, how, where the place or position.

26. LOVERS OF LONLINESS

Brave hearts are they like dullness
Who exceptionally loves loneliness?
Fight with mighty forces of silence
Amidst the dim murk of calmness
Denizens of the deep unfathomable
Lovers of slackness unavoidable
Worshipers of blackness invisible
Men of unquestionably tolerable.
Warriors of frightful solitariness
Speechless speakers of serenity
Heartless hearts of solitude
Murmuring birds of tranquility
Rare of the rarest their greatness
Solitary sailors of the vastness
Reclusive pleaders of emptiness
Indifferent men of worldliness.
Extraordinary men of Humanity
Cloistered men of Individuality
Accursed men of social beauty
Having charismatic personality.
Who exclusively loves loneliness
Either men of uncommonness or
Men of commonness in a sense
Lack of common commonsense.

27. A GIFT TO MANKIND

Human's identity a divine entity with variation and heredity
What a gift to mankind in society the preserver of humanity
Humans distinguished creatures in God's creation
Quite special than animals' features in gradation
Emotions from heart expressed open without hesitation
A weapon to humanize people solemn socialization
Men with command of language mesmerize audience
One and all bound to come to compromise ambience
Let it mingles with others without suspect or prevention
More use more culture widens the prospect of globalization
Humans be dumb and dull without a language
No world of necessity newness we can explore to reach
What a beautiful gift of God to mankind
A language always enriches a superb mind.

28. SPICES OF KINDNESS

Trait of godliness vested on humans to follow
But devoid of human heart reigns with blow
Open mind, open heart forever remains
As icon of highness enriched with kindness
Greed and desires makes one heartless
How can he or she be selfless?
Kindness never grows without magnanimity
Love for others without any return is humanity
Kindness as natural as shower of rains
Never comes by force or under aching pains
Where there's a heart there's life to feel and realize
Life is for life to share and care not to penalize
Unless we sow the seeds of close affection
Nothing be expected to reap the crops of cultivation.

29. ORISON

Orison from the very core of heart
Opens the gate of dilemma fast
Drives towards the path of peace
Fetches the eternal bliss
A talisman to expel the inner devil
Before I know my calmness reveals
A power to mingle with eternity
Makes me serve for solidarity
A bridge to connect the realm of Almighty
Empowers to meet ensuing adversity.

30. DUTY IS REAL GURU

Duty not just action to accomplish
Not just promises to fulfill
Or responsibility to shoulder
The best teacher to guide forever
Though a means of making livelihood
Duty enlivens pensive mood.
Duty shows me the mistakes already committed
Accordingly guides me from wrong deeds prohibited
In duty come ups and downs, failure or success
Teaches me to follow the right process
Warns me, advises me, moulds me in various places
Makes me known all about my weaknesses
Makes me understand the worth of things
Looked down upon by others on dealings
Duty my light, my courage and knowledge
Frees me from the clutches of savage
My anchor, my holder, my moulder
Makes me immortal even my death to ponder
If you really wish not to visit any hospital do your duty
Duty will care, heal, and nourish you with peace and agility
If you want to become rich and powerful do your duty
Duty will enrich you with imperishable prosperity
Do or die but do and die without any foul
Duty will indeed immortalize thou soul
Make your Duty as your Guru with love, affection and devotion

Duty will definitely love you, offer you what you need

31. APOLOGY WITHOUT REGRET

Appealing apology changes one's mind to think over consideration
Shows a new path of progression with hope and confidence
Apology without regret wears a mask of mala fide intent
Nobody can understand how easily someone to content
Apology without changed behavior a manipulation
Like shedding crocodile's tears a pretentions
Without any weapon heart tears apart a retaliation
If you remain silent to bear unwanted toleration a hallucination.
Apology is not apology unless repentant to modification
Be aware of masquerades certainly driven to misconception.

32. THE BRAVE

The brave are the ones who always speak the truth
Till the last breath of life
Who can raise the voice against injustice?
Fight for solidarity and divine peace.
The brave are the ones who never desire excess
Live for others and leave ways for others to progress
Keep one's heart open to greet all in process
Nowhere or nobody can suppress as blessed with god's grace.
The brave are the ones who controls five senses
Can tackle all situations applying commonsense
Ready to compromise and adjust not to disgrace
Both friends and foes, smiles and tears they heartily embrace
The brave are the ones who are self satisfied
Neither in happiness overjoyed nor in fear sorely horrified
Dedicate themselves for the betterment of society
For the sake of mother land, language, culture and humanity.

33. HUMANS REAL DUTY

If humans are humane in reality
Human ambience breeds humanity
Something, somewhere or somebody cannot be taught
Rather acquired around us which are sought
Let emotions flow without any pressure
Crying, seeing, feeling, touching, smelling measure
Think not past, worry not future, present is treasure
What you see before you not always ranger
Let doubts deleted by faith of the eraser
Then does come humanity's pleasure
Some divine duty makes a man noble
Magnanimity makes him humble
Remaining without the track of manhood
Never let anyone in any situation brood
Concentration of senses together brings eternal bliss
If humans real duty from mind and heart never miss
Simplicity the key to the sustenance of humanity
Let's follow the path of bravery and brevity.

34. SONGSTER

Creator of songs
Artistically sings
Melodiously sung
Heart core songs.
Prolific songsters
Great entertainers
Apt master blasters
Myriads mind manures.
Heart captures
Mind raptures
Soul nurtures
Life cultures
Mesmerizing magic
Hypnotizing music
Beating of heart
Lifelong impart.

35. MAN OF NO TALES

Men of no tales are fair
Devoid of lies and cares.
Men of no tales are rare
Nevertheless they care.
Men of no tales express
What they never suppress.
Men of no tales are story
They can create mystery.
Men of no tales wonders
Wonders of all wonders
Men of no tales are morals
Though mortals still immortals.
Men of no tales are narrators
Tell the story of the Creator.

36. HOW TO BECOME BETTER PERSON

No higher education with high degree qualification

Makes anyone, anywhere a better person

Not even name, fame, property whatever in possession

Unless and until he or she can closely understand any situation.

Not all sweet words devoid of pretention or hallucination

Not all lies are lies full of poison, unless hurt one's emotions

Not all creations meaningful or purposeful to everyone

What good for you not bad for someone

Better persons are those who know their weakness or limitation

The best are those who accept all without selection

Both bad and good equally fills the needs or expectations

Actions are better than words to bring perfection.

37. BYGONE LOVE

Gone is the love still reeling in mind?
How can I forget bygone love of my life?
Love that so natural sprouted without effort
Bloomed on the petals of special liking unhurt.
Gently steadily grew like crescent moon
Amidst the humdrum of business driven to boon.
Aroma of love spread in the wind of mind
Time space never hides truth from mankind
A magnet of attraction tied us with mirth
We did forget our age color date of birth
Love is blindness tries not to see before
Love is itself beauty divine scenes and sights galore.
No line of control distanced us to mingle
To share each other the heart and soul ripple
No love of bygone days, today or tomorrow stale or pale
Love is truth love is victory always fresh and cozy as well
Love never fails, never betrays those who love by heart
Whole universe knells down before pure love no doubt.

38. COMPASSION

Searching hidden expression to recognize
Voluntary help unconditional to sympathize
The suffering inside heart to vividly read
To execute magnanimity for taking heed
That's the way of compassion, mind to feed.
Life without compassion like a vast desert
Where no lives survive to see the light
Feeling of the severity of pain feels others' ache
Can understand the position of fish out of water
An inner voice of heart comes out to stand for the helpless
Where and where resides compassion to heal the cheerless
Nobody can create a beautiful life or purchase one, not a passion
But can rescue one out of danger with a little compassion
For which nothing lost, nor ended, nor taken way with ransom.

39. MATTERS A LOT

Monkeys know not the value of coconut
For the blind the mirror in their front
Bananas taste sour when pigs are offered
Homes unsafe when own people in theft involved.
Gold seems brass when in open market sold
And brass indeed baffle if colored in gold.
Matters a lot if ignored by people we value
That teaches us something in lieu.
Offering something to someone voluntarily or by force
Demean the value of offer and offered both of course.

40. THE WAY ONE SPEAKS

Words are very powerful that can demolish the tower of love and peace
Friends turn foes in no time with the way one speaks when can't relish
Sarcastic way to present thoughts often leads to conflict
Life of purpose so trifling when the words of relatives many hearts afflict
Be aware of words you are going to pass over somebody
Leaves like arrows once come out never returns to anybody
Tears the heart apart can never be recovered to body
Like the running water rushes down ahead not at all back to the root
Sarcastic words once passing from mouth no chance to sprout
Like the burning fire it severely burns the tree of family group
Sometimes erect thousand walls of hatred and fright
In between two souls made for each other fight however they be upright
The way one speaks makes the difference matters a lot
Let's be economic in words to say something on the spot
Poisonous and contagious is sarcastic words of humans
Better to stay far away from such sweet enemy and bitter friends.

41. BETRAYAL

Man betrays man being a bossom friend
To betray is human to believe is divine trend
Man is the enemy of man who cares much
No less inferior than wild animal as such
Man loves for his own self
Recklessly accumulates pelf
To make is sublime to break offensive
Man can go any extent being destructive
A dog can repay what you have paid
Man does regret when he is approached.
Unlike a beast man is a man betraying to man
More wise more foolish innate nature of human.

42. MAKE YOUR LIFE POETIC

Life is replete with similes and metaphors

Melody, music, magic regularly prosper to decipher

Mellifluous are the voices, sound and word pictures confer

Effulgent hues twisted in its mixture and texture offer

Language of expression, worldwide communication

Makes one laugh and cry with overflow of emotions

Rhymes and rhythm profusely evolves to chant rejuvenation

Hallucinations fails to erect the citadel of self realization

Life is a poetry, recite it for your gratification

Read by heart, can heal the wound of tension

Dive into the heart of poetry it can move you the whole universe

However unknown, unseen and untrodden or far away.

43. HOME OF MY LIFE

Family, friends and society all are pillars of my life
The edifice of my home stands on the foundation of love
Myself the mason of my own mansion
Made me toil over years of sweat and blood
Filling the store house with the pelf of compassion
Unending source of stream the whole mankind to flood
What I am and how I am the result of dedication
Now let me renovate with resplendent hues of actions
Painted by the mosaic colors of emotions with passion
Let me bedeck each chamber with the ornaments of humanity
And embellish the home with the rainbow of solidarity.
To make the helpless sanguine of hope and smiles
To enliven their life to carry on journey miles after miles
I wish nobody be deprived of solace, peace and prosperity.

44. SERAPHIC SMILE

In your absence
Your seraphic smile
Dances before me
I forget who am I
In my sorrows of loneliness
Feeds me happiness
Your seraphic smile
Oozing my mind in calmness
In my pleasure of success
Limits my excess
Your seraphic smile
Without letting me be reckless
In my failure of consciousness
Blows the horn of call
Your seraphic smile
Never let me befall.

45. EYES

Eyes the loveliest and softest sensitive part of human life
The best similes and metaphors for poems to write
The stars and the moon in the azure sky
Sees the verdant earth staying far away.
Eyes not only behold things beautiful
But also retains memories unforgetfull
Love, hate, lies, truth displayed on their screen
Anger, hunger, thirst, wish palpably seen
The ugly are avoided to explore the beauty
The slightly quite allowed to glorify dignity.
The flower of joy blooms in its petal
The rivulet of tears flows from the channel.
Eyes, however, say nothing
Can vividly express anything.

46. DREAMS TO WISH

Some dream I have I wish come true
A society where both man and woman equally blessed
With the same grace of Almighty, so no hatred
Where let old helpless parents be worshipped
Where no betrayal in love, words or action
Where no corruption, no exploitation or no molestation
Let the buds bloom without any spoliation
Where live the gods and goddesses in diverse incarnation
Let humans travel on the highway of positivity
Explore the world to search the best of fertility
Understand oneself and others with the perception of maturity
Let things grow in their own way to pluck the fruits of humanity
Dreaming a realm of peace and prosperity
Where people are devoid of anger, envy and enmity
Far from the madding crowd of selfishness and gravity
Spreading the fragrance of equality, justice and fraternity
Dreaming a heart replete with symphony of feelings
A heart open and frank for all with cheers and smiling
A mind with broad and heightened sensibility
To comprehend the plea, plight of world community.

47. LOVE YOU

LOVE you as a mother loves her child
As animals to the green forest even wild
Love you as the moon loves the lily
As the rising sun to the lotus in glee.
Love you as a flower loves honey bees
As life to life and to all things the breeze.
Love you as a shopkeeper loves his customers
As the peacocks to the first showers of clouds
My love never dies even after my death
As life never stay away without breath.
How can make you understand I love you
More than my life, I think no need of any cue.
Love is love is love, a diamond forever
Above, over, under or beneath everywhere in you I discover.

48. A LADDER TO THE SKY

WHY I need a ladder to the sky
Which is unseen in the high?
Rather to gather piles of work step by step
If I don't help me how can anybody help?
Life is itself a ladder having so many steps
I have to climb one after the other life be safe.
Nobody ensure what will come next beyond
Why should I waste my time for a ladder to be built?
Let me render for whatever assigned to me
That will crest me high up in the sky.
Little by little makes everything vast
Nothing can be achieved with hurry and moving too fast.

49. WORLD OF FANTASY

Different from so called world
Beyond reality unbelievable
Words have magic to flow
Like a river murmuring unspeakable.
World of fantasy the world of ecstasy
Reveals the truth of purity and delicacy
Mind-blowing grace of aesthetic supremacy
Dreams come true with love and intimacy.
World of fantasy imitation of creation so appealing
Beyond one's imagination artistic inspiring
Takes the lead of man's maturity with perfection
Enriching the eternal sublime impression.

50. LIARS

A chameleon is a liar who alters hue to tweak
A person, place, action or time in freak
Something happens unusual before someone can comprehend
But a liar easily escapes as he can apprehend.
Liars are black clouds engulf the mighty sun
Frighten the heart of divine mind in fun
When caught lies red-handed, throw the trap of flattery
Pleased are the listeners enormously recharged with witty battery.
Liars are the sweet enemy and bitter friends in disguise
Sole duty they perform many a men to mobilize
Towards the direction of falsehood and devilish
Adroitness
But defeated in the grand finale of righteousness.
Liars are the horse riders in hand having no reins
Like thundering clouds in vacuum rumble with no rains
Build the castles of pyre in the graveyard
To hide their face under the veil of shame and hatred.

51. ANGER IS BAD COUNSELLOR

Memory collapsed when anger takes place

Presence of mind flies away

One forgets one's place and position

Darkness clouded all over perception

In a moment of space and time

Personality turns to matter of fun to rescind

Burns like fire the essence of life

Dragging away to unwanted strife

Man of anger a bad Counselor

Seeds of hatred sprouted in heart's corner

Spreads like a poison tree all around

Killing the lives of innocent and humble in mound.

52. TEENAGE LOVE

Raw fruits, hanging on bowers, more tasty than ripe ones
A stage of greenness, quite ingenuous, looking fresh
A mirthful game like hide and seek to play
A moment of enjoying life in full bloom to sway
Teenage love a dream to dream without nights
Makes the teenagers soar in the sky of heights
Sometimes pushes them to dungeon of desires
Where grimly suffocated they are to respire.
Taste of newness so sweet however risky
In scorching summer as we need a whisky
Path of teenage love illusively smooth but rocky
Something lost in terms of gaining being choosy.

53. ROSE, THY NAME IS SANCTITY

Resplendent flower of miracles

Oasis in the desert of hatred

Sweeps away the filth of obstacles

Emblem of love wholly sacred

A bridge between the two souls

To easily reach the shores

Overcoming all huddles

A hypnotic creation with attraction

Enables the two sides to come closer

Even stone heart agrees to surrender

All his or her trauma to ponder

Over the uniqueness of rose in each colour

Rose, thy name is sweetness, hotness, smartness, eagerness

How one can refuse thy tenderness

Rose, thy name is sanctity

In your presence melts away the snow of rudeness

Diamond like sparkles in the hands of lovers looking celebrity.

Blessed are those who really embrace you in practicality

In sleep, in dream, in words, in action in thy vivacity

Lucky are you being the superb creation of Almighty.

54. SCARS INSIDE OUTSIDE

New twigs born if a tree is cut
Any wound heald even if burnt
But no glue can join the broken pot
Aa scars inside heart undeleted spot
There stands an unforgettable hut
No talent of mankind stops the rot.
But life is not possible without having a naevus
Every mark in life comes with a purpose
Even moon in the sky not void of stigma
Beyond human thoughts to know this enigma
Life with some scars inborn intimacy
As lovely as childhood innocence
A black mole on the cheek of a lady
Centre of attraction multiplies beauty
Rose blooming on thorny stem pretty
Tasteless water quenches the thirsty
How can you scale the scars in haste?
Without going deep to gauge the best
Some scars visible some invisible
Some are chewed some ever tasted
Some are embracing some negligible
Some detested some eagerly hosted
Life and scars magically indivisible
With good grace both highly vested.

55. FIRST LOVE

The first of the first anything, anytime, anywhere
Engraved in mind and heart forever
The advent of a first son or daughter eternal mirth of motherhood
The much awaited desire enlivens her mood however bitter or crude
Falling of first showers of rains soothes pain striking land
Rejoiced the moment of joy in childhood hand in hand
Meeting of first time first place colorfully paints
The lovers and beloveds in the marble of love with unfaded scent.
The first income of a worker brings unfathomable delight
Motivates towards righteousness and service right
First letter from first lover racks in the museum of heart
Each word each line day by day derives plenty of sense to impart
First caress of lover excites like electric current
Makes one sail jovially in the boat of love like water torrent.

56. HOME COMING

The joy of home coming
Undoubtedly indescribable
When two lives mingle
With heart and soul
The path gets shortened
Travels become enjoyable
Lightened is the blue sky
To pave the way of passerby comfortable
All pains turn to pleasure
Destination comes closer
When accompanied by
A lovely life partner.

57. NO PAIN, NO GAIN

New twigs burgeon when the old ones chopped
If no devastations, nothing new to be hoped
Seeds under soil lose contours to sprout
When something in, something must be out.
If there is no falling, no rising of leaves
Hence, for loss or gain no reasons to grieve
Edifice of newness stands on the base of ruination
Let's watch and wait things with rumination.
If there's no emptiness, there's no fulfillment
There's no fulfillment if there's no complement
Pain and pleasure twin flames of life in closer
In absence of one, the other you can never measure.

58. WHAT FLOWERS TEACH US

Flowers born with fragrance gift of Almighty

So is mankind with humanity

Humans die for their own cause

When flowers for other's cause

Does a flower feel pride of its beauty

But a man does forget his duty.

Flowers with different colors teaches a lot

Following them one can make one's own lot.

Dedicated are flowers for its lord

Great shame that man betrays his own god.

Sacrificed life still flowers never care but cheer

No human being surrenders faults here.

No flower preserve anything for itself

Corrupted are humans hesitate not to rape.

Regretted to see the gap between the two creations

Let's introspect the future of civilization.

59. TWO FORCES OF THE TIME

Mother India proud to have two sons
On Second October engraved on the marble of civilization
Two forces of the Time did shine
Nation gladly chanted chimes
Grew like crescent moon in the India's sky
Surrendered the mighty British forces
Before the two forces
The amalgam of strength, courage and knowledge
Love, peace and harmony to blaze
Throughout the Empire of Mother India
Both are two in one
Men of simplicity and intelligence
Immortal souls for reverence
Men of humility and confidence
Victory bowed down for credence
Men of humbleness and nobleness
Rendering service with righteousness
Men of honesty and integrity
Deeds dedicated for solidarity
Power of tolerance and perseverance
Stimulated for better governance
Far from envy, jealousy and violence
Opted the weapon of nonviolence
Men of morality and coherence

Men of unity in diversity

Men of stability in chaotic futility

Erected the base of free nation

To stand the edifice of future generation.

60. UNSEEN LIGHT

Light inside the core of poverty
Unseen, unwanted but leads to creativity
Emptiness gets enriched with generosity
Farfetched thoughts flown to humanity.
Light inside the deep and dark silence
Enlightens the azure of classic productivity
Sometimes garnering from reminiscence
Often from the world of mosaic activity.
Light inside the heart consoles the depressed
Makes one cry and smile to embrace the suppressed
Sings the song of life to rejoice the oppressed
With the emotions of spontaneity to the blessed
Unseen light lying hidden inside the arena of slavery
Nobody desires to stay in such land of ivory
Which only prohibits the intruders of excessive monopoly
Commands over the denizens of slavery to reside in own grocery.
Unseen is the light of hearts of illiterate and innocent
But never ever betray the so called literate and intelligent
Instead are deliberately deceived by the percipient
As if born to be underestimated, often being subservient.

61. ENVY

Euphoria of intolerance the mother of envy to bear
Other's success story never can hear
Luxury and happiness begrudging affluence to cheer
Men of envy are men of their own enemy highly tended to fear.
Neurodivergence of bitter blessings and sweet curses
Wholeheartedly from core of heart rushes
Paint the color of vigorous words to shine
Before the curtain a well wisher who niggardly whine.
Vain and void of ebullient wishes sounding amiable
Verity vapors in the noise of encomium seeming amicable
Vanity flattered, words crackered with a song of futility
Vested with enigmatic smiles of Gail and gaiety.
Yielding wan hope to believe in eyes may not be devoid
Man of envy in life more poisonous than poison, possibly avoid.

62. POWER OF EDUCATION

Education means not write or read words, sentence

It liberates from the chains of ignorance and innocence

Enables to read persons, places and character

Comprehends situation, circumstances and happenstances

Stops those stopping the flow of advancement

Exposes those thinking ill of others in development

Education brings a change in everything

Refines, reforms, reshapes, remoulds the inner self

To independently stands hale and bold to save something safe.

Education shows the right path to follow

Right things to humanize the world of sorrows

Weapons to vanquish the enemy of stupidity

Marching forward to conquer the land of futility

Opens the gate of newness however impossible

Explore the vastness of wisdom durable

Helps extending hands for solving problems

Men of education wherever go gain acclaim

A tool to make things colorful like rainbow

Stands like banyan tree to spread shades of shadow

Builds a shelter for the traveler on the way to destination

Caters the needs of the time to fulfill with confirmation

Without education life is like a lifeless log of wood

Humans never attain the golden stage of manhood.

63. WHERE ARE YOU DEAR FREEDOM

Where are you dear freedom?

In your absence I am in humdrum

Captivated I am in my own kingdom

I wish you had definitely come

And rescue from mountainous boredom.

Oh, my dear freedom of speech

Do you think me away from speechless speech?

Bridge collapsed, now how do I reach?

How can I win, rough is the playing pitch?

I wish everything went without a hitch.

Where are you dear freedom?

Come and liberate from serfdom

Let me regain the lost wisdom

I think you will never abandon

Must you keep me away from a random?

Where are you my dear freedom of wanderlust?

Why left me alone in the darkness of thrust

Hope you will not make me a burst

Let me rise like phoenix from ashes and dust

I know you are not yet lost

64. MONSOON FARMING

Nature is magnanimous to offer everything
For everyone everywhere anytime favoring
Tiny creatures to massive man and animals to exist
So does to humble farmer's monsoon farming to subsist.
Much awaited hopes and confidence of cultivators
Caters the need of the time as motivators
Nature preserves the monsoon in her lap
In time releases the same for farmers to cope.
Hearts of the rustics bounce in delight
In the advent of monsoon ready to alight
Tiller's intelligencer turns up with good news
To warm up the farmers whose mind out of fuse.
A source of rapture runs through the innocent mass
New light of trust and assurance peeps to flash
Monsoon farming makes them a class
To provide life to millions on the Earth's surface.

65. OLYMPIC: DREAM OF SPORTSMAN

An internationally organized platform for worldwide sportsman
For own race and nation to fetch name and fame
Individual becomes the national and international property
Crossing the circumference of horizon beyond the narrowness and negativity.
The pearl or diamond hidden inside the interior slum or village
Discovered the Olympic and presents in the frontline page
Many a flowers of sportsman however faded but shine
In wordless applause the whole world chimes in rhyme.
Staunch will power and determination takes them to destination
Millions of dreams peep through the window of passion
Outside support and assistance enables them keeping the journey on
Days are gone but remained some remnants unforgotten.
Olympic the last dream of every national or international player
Toil and sweat over years of severe pain and pleasure
Drives the uncommon one to get down in the wondrous realm
The world picks the best up from the zillions of awaited flame.
After all the Olympiads deserve a chance of amassing wealth
Besides the name and fame the unexpected rushes to their feet till death
Olympic of life crests the Himalayas of impossibility
Along with myriads of dreaming and enchanting prosperity.

66. LIFE AND DEATH

Relay Racers are Life and Death
One ends the race where the other starts
To complete the game of life
Under the supervision of the Guide
Running within the same track
Heartily supporting each other
They know the race be failure
Without one's favor and fervor.
Unerring chemistry have they to cope
Both are complementary to one another to hope
Staunch believers having deep rapport
One leaves other to live, the other lives to leave
Dealings so consummated no one can deceive.
No betrayal, no hatred, no greed between them to conceive.

67. PARADISE

A place of serene, tranquil setting quite appealing
Where no pain of sorrows or suffering
No sign of havoc or panic vehemently appalling.
A place of love, peace, harmony and unity
No hatred, anger, distinction rules in reality.
A place of equality, fraternity and justice
Where each other share, care in bliss
A place of truth, nonviolence
Where unseen are the wrong deeds of liars, violence
A place of kindness, forgiveness
Drenched with the showers of holiness
A place of understanding, compromise
E where everybody possesses the power to realize.
A place of joy and happiness, goodness
Surrounded by the fence of sweetness.
A place of honesty, integrity and sanctity
Where all stand for the sake of solidarity
A place of beauty, tenderness, homeliness
Pervades with the fragrance of friendship and closeness
A place where no discrimination of caste, creed, color or race
All are equal in all respect the sameness to embrace.
Not a place or palace a feeling of godliness
A state of mind to rejoice sublime newness.

68. MIND

Mind is like a computer set
Restored unlimited data to offset.
Mind is like a piece of blank paper to fill up
Let's in the annals of history posterity to follow up.
Mind a piece of land needs to be cultivated day by day
Let the land be tilled with the plough of reading every day.
Mind a powerful magnate to attract
All you embrace and hug capture in fact.

69. I MISS YOUR LULLABY

Days, nights, months and years are gone
But your lullaby still unforgotten
The moment I was obstinate to take food
The moment I was naughty to go to bed
Your lullaby from your sweet voice hypnotized
What a magic and melody incorporated
The spell of lullaby never be segregated
From you and your lullaby that I really missed.
Still I remember your lullaby reeling
How can I say " goodbye" ? smiling
Till my last breath of life listening
Which took away my all strife relieving.
Incomparable the song whispering in silence
Unmatched, unparallel cream of resilience
Fountain of pliability showered incessant
Filtering my heart of remorse complacent.

70. LIFE IS JUST THE WINK OF AN EYE

Life is natural, life is spontaneous

So fabulous but miraculous

The way it grows, the way it moves habitual

Runs its flow unhampered typical

Nobody knows its appearance or disappearance

Neither waits anything nor leaves countenance

Amidst the falling and rising of wink

Occurs something inevitable to sink

Intermingles with the depth of lore to realizeA

But unsure life after or before to surmise

Yes life is just the wink of an eye saying many more

What will happen nobody foresee or foretell mine nor your

71. LIFE IS REAL

Life is real, life is natural
Colorful and beautiful
More meaningful, more purposeful
Live life earnestly so enjoyable
If used fairly becomes most valuable
Let life grow to fill the hollow
Life is present needs to follow
Evidence the past to make future strong
Though short, a great lesson for the throng
Learn it, teach it share it, care it to glow
Keeping in mind the process steady and slow
Life is water drink it, life is food take it to feed
Waiting the hungry and the thirsty to plead.

72. SILENT SPECTATOR

No human under the sun is perfect
Common in life to commit a mistake
No mistakes, no rectification to make
Nothing to happen as we wanted.
When wrong deeds leads to injustice
Nobody can raise voice against mal service
And stayed tuned to misdeeds
Being eyewitness to this
Throat of justice then and there chocked in deed.
Just to be silent spectator a greater injustice
Than the wrong doers induced to accomplish
Detrimental to society far from the world of justice
If so then what to speak of the novice.

73. MEANING OF LIFE

Life is so beautiful to enjoy
Merriment to heartily rejoice
A colorful rainbow to embrace
An art of living, a divine grace.
Life a purpose to serve
A source of diverse job
A word of myriads of synonyms
Replete with homonym and antonym.
Life is temporary but likely to be eternal
Promoted by righteous service universal
A great lesson to teach indeed
If mind be far away from greed.
Life is a golden opportunity
Never comes again and again
A dream of all possibility
Gain emerges out of pain.
Indefinite and imperfect, nobody can define
More illustration, more meaning
Day by Day it takes time to get refined
Life is for caring, sharing and above all rupturing.

74. WHAT A TEACHER IS

A warrior to face every bit of challenge
Bold enough to defuse enemy's revenge
A messenger to serve valuable message
To the whole universe with coverage
A leader to lead the team to success
A processor to present all the process
A guide to guide the obstinate in deed
To build the nation he always takes heed
A friend to cooperate the best in need
Eager to share feelings not to bleed
A master to train the newcomers well
In everybody's hearts he does ever dwell
A speaker to speak the truth to handle
All situations emerging out in bundle
A singer to mesmerize the students
Being tranquillizer to pacify so prudent
A narrator to narrate the naked truth
In respective of caste creed of youth
A dreamer to envisage the golden future
Builds a shelter to save ensuing torture
A rapturer to make everyone rapturous
Smiles and makes others smile continuous
A foreteller to warn all to be conscious
To explore the unknown the miraculous
A researcher to search the novel ideas

For the generations to come
A scientist to invent new criteria
To construct an indestructible kingdom
A discoverer to discover the hidden talents
The need of the hour people's desire
A reformer to reform the social trends
Necessary to uphold the mirror fair
A well wisher to think the betterment
Of learners individual social flair
A motivator for motivate excitement
A balm to assuage the ache of disappointment
A reshaper to reshape remould character
Heading the risk of danger in amazement
A Nurturer to nurture the mankind with lore
For good his successors bound to adore
A nurse to treat the wound of curiosity
Enthusiasm, perseverance in entirety
A doctor to diagnose symptom of failure.
Enable him to take right strategy for winners
A referee to play the game to the players
Dedicating time strength of trumpet blare
A worshipper of knowledge and courage
A technician to take the distant mileage
And what not a teacher is
Can he be out of reach?

75. SWEETNESS OF COLOUR

Color of peace densely whitens the world wide panorama of its kind
Shadowed with calmness and tranquility to wrap the mankind
Color of love showers upon white dove
To enliven earth with affection resolved.
Color of wisdom makes one tenderly polite and highly noble
Wins every heart when humans simply humble, escaped of troubles
Color of imagination painted mosaic word pictures of emotions
Man to poet, readers to writers obviously tempted by creation
Color of humanity the true color of humankind to allure
Man becomes humane when we all remind the cause of failure
Color of kindness brightens the color of human to humanize
Color of forgiveness heightens the sensibility of man to recognize
Color of sacrifice surrenders gravity and vanity, complexity and diversity
Let the whole world be colored with solidarity eternal divinity
Color of song sings the song of life
Brushing up the faded color of strife.

76. WOMEN EMPOWERMENT

Incomplete is God's creation without a woman
It's time not to condemn
Imperfect is man without a woman's rise
It's time to rid her not to criticize
Insufficient is man's service
No woman no peace
Indiscipline is the life of mankind
It's time to value her presence behind
Impossible to dream without a night
Without thread how can you fly the kite?
Ugly is the society in her absence
As if we had life without sense
Oasis in the desert is woman
Fragrance of the flower is woman
Shadow of a tree is woman shower of rain is woman
It's time to ponder over her ensuing domain
Unaware of own self and ease
Untired of duties and responsibilities
How can you treat she is frailty
How can you spoil her beauty?
The image of fertility and chastity, nobility and humility
It's time to feel her divinity, magnanimity
Love her support her worship her integrity
The goddess of sacrifice recognizes her identity.

77. BORDERLESS WORLD

World a beautiful creation with no boundary
Civilization by mankind needs a fence primary.
Not among the people only but among the relatives
Make a wall to isolate themselves being no cooperative.
Humanity is at stake due to his or her selfishness
Nobody's business has become everybody's business.
Jealousy, envy, enmity root cause of more expectations
Humans are no more humans to be humane without hesitation.
Humans can go any extent for fulfilling own satisfaction
Unaware of one's role assigned busy for interruption
To alarmingly increase own name fame and recognition
Forgetting that nothing is ours nothing will go with us
Just passing the sojourn we have to depart the cosmos.
Why then this competition, corruption and manipulation and for
what
The world is meant for us but not ours to use as we like to part.
Why this boundary for whom after a while they depart
We are just some day's guest to enjoy life with comfort being smart.
O poor creatures let's ponder over the matter that matters
Live and let live others sharing love and peace for life is to live better.

78. LEAVE NOT ME ALONE

Excuse me dear for a last chance you hear

From the core of my heart I promise I will bear

Everything from top to bottom you just stay near

With me helping to rectify my flaws to cheer.

Let me swear in the name of God to you endear.

How can I say I am not what you think so far?

You have seen my anger not my love yet deeper

Forget not that love lies not only in love but in anger

If there's distance there's closeness forever

Try to watch the nearness of sun and lotus as lovers.

This time I assure wouldn't make you hopeless

Be cheerful, sanguine of me being fearless

My dear you remember am not so careless

Your place is always inside my heart god's grace

If I were Hanuman I would show you tearing chest to impress.

Earnest request leave not me alone

Stay with me to rejoice once again

Let flowers bloom in our garden

Leave not my land of love barren

We are made each other in our heaven

Your presence is my confidence

My strength, my love so dense

Your absence is my weakness

Shall be lost in your long silence

Thou are my desire intense
Leave not me alone my life's life
Beat of my heart soul of my life
Push not me into the pit of strife
Let's be a class be a unique type
For you are special spices of my life

79. MEN OF LETTERS

Abundantly flatter sweet in sound
Like birds flutter round and round
Round the clock all around found
Mankind's betterment aptly mould.
Men of letters always glitter like gold.
Narrators of stories yet untold
Unacknowledged legislators
Unscientific world inventors
Committed honorary workers
Undoubtedly social reformers
Men of letters gavel of glamour.
Decorators of literary parlor.
Lifelong dreamers to dream
For the hopeless a gleam
For the depressed a beam
For the oppressed freedom
The world a unique kingdom
Golden and ideal home.
Avid readers of apprehension
Intent listener of inner voices
Voluble speakers of universalisation
Prolific writer of eternal creation
Men of comprehension
Establish global peace unison
Messenger of unification

Harbinger of motivation
Sources of inspiration
Advocates of modification.
Blessed are they alone
Gifted with power of creation
Singers to sing melodious song
Painters to paint picture of words
Architectures to design the write
Artists to worship each art's right
Friends, philosophers and guides
In their eyes nothing can hide.
Men of letters men of devotion
Strive to mend all erring action.

80. UNENDING MUSIC OF EARTH

The place where we live in a storehouse of music and melody.

Unending source of love and rapture

Morn to night and night to mourn audible to everybody

The song of joy and sorrow the earth has mixed feature.

Morning starts with the music of bird's twittering

And ends with the chirruping of offspring in the evening.

The entire day filled with the melody of the roaring of rustling and bustling

Somewhere beasts somewhere birds flapping and clapping and hustling.

No rest of the music of earth incessantly runs

One after the other groups by groups takes their turns.

Whistling of the wind makes ripples in the leaves to dance

Earth looks like a vast stage of concert with several entrance

Silence plays hide and seek with the darkness at night

For prey nocturnal animals and birds come out to fight

To win over the weak destined to fall in prey

With some tricks some escapes and the Lord to pray.

No stop of music and melody in any situation in any season

Her lovely creations keep playing on with so many reasons

All things living and non-living co operate each other

To sing the song of Mother Earth with enthusiasm together.

O human beings let's listen to the unending diverse music

In spite of diversity look how everything positive and optimistic

That teaches the whole mankind to follow her lesson majestic
Let's us learn that everybody has rights to hear earth's music
Spontaneously mesmerizing magnanimously fantastic
Have a cosmic attitude for all hopefully without being self centric.

81. AN OFFICER OR A PEON

An officer or a Peon whoever is great
Officer an officer, peon a peon matter straight
But world of difference between the two
One's position so high the other low too
May be in education, vocation or rank
In prestige honor social official not prank
May be in money, power, name and fame
Luxury, scale of standard or choice of game
Despite diversity lies some uniformity in guise
In between subordinate and authority
Both belong to the race of humanity
An officer great in his place so is peon
One deprived of chance other blessed
Can the officer run the office without a peon?
Can the officer place the files in order?
How can he keep the office neat and clean
Why the officer needs the help of a peon
Inside the office gives a reason enough
To weigh the greatness of officer and peon.

82. HOUSE WIFE

Quenching thirst with the sweat of labor
For her family she is unconditional lover
No wages no leave an honorary worker
Only out of love, of heart from very core
No vacation no commission no more
For she is the utmost promising caretaker
To one and all members a good listener
Alas ! Everybody pays deaf ear to her
Morn to night being a well wisher
Earnestly calls the Almighty in her prayer
Not for her own self but for others welfare
No claim no vanity no greed no anger
What an embodiment of a lady in character
Compromise, adjustment cooperation
As if her only foundation, manifestation
Sacrifice, toleration her mighty strength
Service, offering, silence sole wealth
Home minister, prime minister and all in all
With no power, but moon among the stars
A fighter, warrior soldier with no weapons
No rival competitors but much competition
What a noble sober modest host
But rare ladies want to take the post.
Now is the time to pay due honour in sense
For her diligence patience perseverance

Punctuality, sincerity, integrity, loyalty
Honesty, magnanimity and hospitality
Come forward and wish for her longevity.
Every day in calendar a day of observation
Why not a Housewife Day celebration.
For her dreams dedication and passion.

83. MORNING SKY

Morning wakes up with scenic beauty
Painted by the diverse colors of serenity
Each morning comes with fresh start
Fresh air, fresh light, fresh mind pretty smart
Blowing the horn of consciousness
Each moment of life be not emptiness
Morning tears up the heart of darkness
To enlighten the sky of dizziness
Kissing the cheeks of clouds in numbness
Like a coy mistress's carefulness
As morning born from the heart of mighty sun
Time being the mother moulds the mind to run
Nurturing with the food of change however forlorn.
Let the morning sky of each life be abundantly brightened
With the limpid light of fairness highly heightened.

84. FOUR LETTERED WORD

Four lettered word seems plain
No words or phrase can explain.
Four lettered word sweet sound
Neither complex nor compound.
Four lettered word looks simple
As ephemeral as water bubble.
Four lettered word assumes humble
Sometimes tumbles some grumbles.
Four lettered word supposed to be light
However stocky hold not tight with might.
Four lettered word unlimited to alphabet
Still incomplete nobody can illustrate.
Four lettered word born with purposes
The more you derive more it proposes.
Four lettered word indefinite meaning
Person to person quite differentiating.
Four lettered word nothing but an art
How to live and survive it can impart.
Four lettered word full of letters
Some bad, some good some better.
Four lettered word a gift of Almighty
However short so priceless and pretty.
Four lettered word speaks a lot
Whoever unmindful sad his lot.

Four lettered word a melodious song
So sweet, mesmerizing enjoy life long.
Four lettered word a splendid magic
Demonstrates game comic and tragic.
Four lettered word a fantastic music
Addition of rhythm modern and classic
Four lettered word is nothing but life
How meaningful easily you can surmise.

85. PARENTS OF A SON

Glad to have a son
Regarded lucky often
To be parents of a son
Daughters forgotten
Son rises like sun
Think not it a fun
Childhood like morn
Them flashes upon
Hearts inside spark
Sing like a sky lark
The son they mark
The centre of park
Morning glow passes
Noon the youth rushes
Loving bird gushes
Parents they pushes
To the pit of loneliness
Turning to darkness.
Everything seems alike
The world looks heaven
Nothing there shaken
Nothing can happen
All over golden.
Afternoon sets in
Rising sun rests in

Beyond the horizon
Leaving them far
Distance be the bar
Lining East and West
In between parents
Back not advance not
Entangled in fright
Helplessness override
Neither cry not delight.

86. THE WAY WE WERE

I wish the day would come the way we were
That sleepless nights talking over phone
Time never passing words running more and more
To listen sweet voice what a melodious tone.
The day never came to an end without gossiping
As the bubbling river never stops murmuring
The day the park witnessing the meeting
Unaware of the vast gathering.
Different and special was the arrangement of engagement
The spring was pleasant favorable to hail the advent
All sights and scenes seemed as lively as heavenly spirit
Captivated I was in thy benign presence to entreat.
Let me implore under the feet of Almighty
To achieve those golden days of felicity
Let the future be colored by past memories
Life be stripped the blanket of unwanted worries.

87. LIFE IS AN EXAMINATION

All the world is an examination centre vast
Where life is an examination long or short
We are all mere examinees slack or smart
Every day we are tested by an evaluator
Under the supervision of an examiner
Get ready and be prepared to face the test
Enter not into the hall in haste
As early as possible in advance be present
The gate be closed if you are late
The ordeal you have to face alone
What are you doing is not for yours
For someone else to come unknown
Do the best for coming with flying colors
Today is seen tomorrow unseen
Let by gone bye by gone greet presence in.

88. PEN- NOW AND THEN

Like a plough it can till the land of futility
The owner derives pleasure for harvesting fruits of fertility
Incarnated many a form now and then to flow
When everything in slumber, it starts journey to grow.
Swallows the silence and serenity of loneliness
Late hour labor gathers the jewels of genuineness
Hiding himself in the dark of anxiety, pathos and sorrows
Drives the chariot of mighty pen towards filling hollows.
From time to time demonstrating shapes and size makes realize
The whole mankind in gale and gaiety of life, minimize
No power can drag it away from its path
Unforgettable it is to render benevolent service burning in hearth..
Pens now and then handled and manipulated for encouragement
Showering the flowers of magic and music of excitement
Promising love, peace and harmony for humanity
Mighty power to move the mountains immovability .
Melts away the stony heart of people to murmur
Culprits are profusely imposed fines and sure to suffer
Garlands of victory ready to greet the revered warrior
Drastic changes it has seen but never changes character.

89. LET LIFE BECOME

Let life become
A sun to rise and set
Rest not to the rest.
Let life become
A river to flow
To seek own way to follow.
Let life become
A tree to bear fruit
Someone to distribute.
Let life become
A drop of water
Needs to cater.
Let life become
A stable mountain
Immovable in sun and rain.
Life is to become
Make life awesome
Without being quarrelsome.

90. FRIENDSHIP DAY

Limit not the friendship in hello hai, bye bye
Remembering to wish a friend on the eve of day or on the day
Shaking hands or greetings not enough to sway
Stop not to keep up forever the rapport to stay
A day is not enough to celebrate a friendship day
Friendship a deep understanding of the one you love
Where no questions raise, no flattery or praise masked
The ocean of faith where lies the pearl of friendship
A bridge between the two poles to connect relationship
To share and care each other without thinking of hardship
An unconditional likeness of closeness
Inseparable however distant in physical presence
A haven of reciprocation to get rid of loneliness
A lifelong companion to accompany in the journey of sorrows and happiness
No clouds of envy, jealousy and pretention can engulf
The domain of friendship.

91. FAILURE

No man is born perfect by nature
Life is full of success and failure
You can't rise without you fall
Rise and fall, fall and rise makes life's circle.
Embrace Failure and be a superman
If you keep distance nothing hope to gain
Failures bridge all the gaps to perfect
Success comes out when sub sided are defects.
Yes, man can be a man in eyes of Failure
Failure never betrays if you love with valour
Failure teaches how to survive with vigour
Patching the crevices of life galore.

92. HAPPY RAKSHA BANDHAN

I wish everybody had a sister to mollycoddle
Sometimes to riddle, sometimes to twiddle
Sustaining angelic rapport, love and affection
Unconditional, unparallel, undestroyed bond of relation.
A sister's love lets every brother pay respect to other sisters
Never let him think ill of others even behind the curtain's corner
A sister who always reminds a brother of his duty
Who absolutely feels undoubted safety and security.
A sister never cares for any adversity or huddles
With a brother standing for sister's pleasure
A feeling of such a day bridges the gap between brother- sister
Makes a promise to present in time of danger
Happy Raksha Bandhan to all brothers and sisters
Let renew the past glory of habits, customs and culture
Let fraternity survive in the crisis of bond in rapture
Let the world feel proud of having a sister in future.

93. Moment to Remember

Arrived the day of Christmas to celebrate
Love and affection from Him to accumulate
Message of simplicity and humility to circulate
Lighting the Christmas tree to illuminate.
Alighted the angel of bliss and peace
It is in December no one can want to miss
The golden moment of rapture to establish
Without fail let's hug and kiss.
A day of hope and light with assurance
Sacrifices the reason of patience and tolerance
Every year in December fills the hearts of children
With variety of priceless gift to offer again.
Search not anywhere the secrets of success
Neither the market nor the forest to access
Wait not the deep dark night to dream excess
What needed is how you adopt the process .
Arrived the day of Christmas to celebrate
Love and affection from Him to accumulate
Message of simplicity and humility to circulate
Lighting the Christmas tree to illuminate.
Alighted the angel of bliss and peace
It is in December no one can want to miss
The golden moment of rapture to establish
Without fail let's hug and kiss.
A day of hope and light with assurance

Sacrifices the reason of patience and tolerance
Every year in December fills the hearts of children
With variety of priceless gift to offer again.
Search not anywhere the secrets of success
Neither the market nor the forest to access
Wait not the deep dark night to dream excess
What needed is how you adopt the process.

94. BROKEN HEART

Failure in love breaks heart apart
When two souls perpetually depart
When justice bows head before injustice
Busted the heart of divine bliss
When simplicity molested openly
Righteousness easily victimized
When are downtrodden oppressed?
When the culprits declared blameless
Twisted the heart of tenderness
Once heartbroken nothing can join
Except unconditional love, affection and kindness
Maximum expectations minimize confrontations
Minimum you desire with maximum satisfaction.

95. WHEN YOU LOVE

When you love, you are matured to understand
As innocent as child who never betray
When you love more than you, you believe
No place, person or time to deceive.
Love neither says nor claims but unconditionally renders
No mighty power under the sun hinders
Trust, hope attraction, a bond of relation
Does not seek or wait for time, place or action.
When you love
You dedicate yourself and your selfishness
Conscious of even a little bit of closeness
Too much caring to look after littleness.
Love cannot see your beauty or ugliness
Never count down the returning of happiness
Never mind your absence or presence.

96. WHO BEING LOVED, IS POOR

Love, love that opens the door
Who being loved is poor?
Love is the reason
For whom it concerns
Love gives light to show
Nothing remains unseen and hollow
Love hates not the fellow
Humans dig out their own furrow
To sow the seeds of sorrow
Harvest the fruits of tomorrow
Love being sweet or sour

97. DAUGHTERS DAY

Daughters are the incarnation of fathers
As sons of mothers
Prestige and beauty together
Resides in them forever
Sources of soberness, stability
Think not them feeble and frail.
More priceless than jwels
More sparkling than pearls
Centre of attraction allures
Angels of wealth and valour.
Oasis in the desert of society
Pivot of character in diverse roles
Like flowers give away magnanimity
Kindness, love, affection with integrity.
Daughters take the lead of humanity
Avoid not them for their frailty
Daughters can fulfill parents' last wish
Sons cannot what daughters accomplish.
Daughters are always compromising
Demand nothing because of understanding
Bridge the gap between two shores
Relates the two unknown souls.
Happy Daughters Day
To all daughters of the world
Complementary to good will

Chariot of society can't run
If daughters are forlorn.
Myself lucky enough to have two princess
Akankshya and Ayushi God's grace.

98. INDEPENDENCE DAY

A day of freedom and happiness
A day of safety and security
A day of pride for equity, equality and fraternity
A day of oneness, togetherness for nation's betterment
Time for promise to do the best for development
A day to introspect the past glory for future enrichment
A day to offer homage to the revered sons of motherland
Salute to the tricolor flag of peace, love and harmony
Let the dreams be fulfilled with invigorating ceremony
A golden chance to repay what we are already paid
An opportunity to share what we have to narrate
A day to feel proud of being free Indian
A day to celebrate the day as the day of victory.
A day of change to stabilize and sustain better governance
Without caring for, agonizing for any happenstances
Let the pen bleed with psalms of humanity
Spreading the fragrance of love and solidarity.

99. BE LIKE A BUTTERFLY

If want to allure the little ones
Be like a butterfly at least once
And be a source of divine bliss
To offer the eternal peace.
If you wish to make life colorful
Be like a butterfly to be cheerful
The centre of attraction be its fickleness
Singing the song of pure innocence.
If you long for love to grace
Be like a butterfly not to leave who embrace
Love each one no matter bad or good
Hug and kiss with no return in every mood.
Sweet and jocund are all small things
Replete with innermost sense of feelings
Most beautiful are the tiny however ephemeral
Leave something for generations perennial.

100. HAPPY NEW YEAR, 2021

A year to greet with abundant delight from my site
Wishing the New Year be happy and prosperous
Some resolutions be made to fulfill in thoughts and actions
Not only for own self but also for others with motivation
Be the year the year of love, harmony and peace
Worldwide to establish with God's gracious and divine bliss
No natural calamities, no socio-economic and political instability
No woman atrocities, no rape and murder, society be devoid of complexity
Let the New Year run without any treachery, backbite
Stand together to raise voice against injustice to fight with might
We are humans to share feelings each other
Must we heartily promise to care one another?
Be social, rational and moral being to serve the mankind
Leaving something memorable, desirable and constructive behind.
Happy, Happy, Happy New Year my dear
Be kind, liberal and helpful to make us cheer.

101. CREDIT YOURSELF

The path you follow
Never be a hollow
The service you render
Forever there to glow
Nights become slow
Dreams to flow
Thoughts be positive
Mission be progressive
If vision is affirmative
Ideas taken constrictive.
Nothing be destructive
All is within you
Stored in plenty too
Why not credit you
All that what you are
Absolutely true.

102. VIRIDITY

Like pearl inside conch
Like musk inside navel
Never, never shown outside
Aroma spread worldwide.
Pregnant with stupidity
Proudly ever say viridity
Turns to cent percent reality
The Sensible pay deaf year
For self centred here
To remain aloof from mere
Loss of near and dear
Putting aside out of fear.
Unlike the conscious
May be unconscious
But never be injudicious
To fulfill own purpose
Dare to dive into dungeon
To rescue unseen, unknown
As they purely innocent
Know not what will happen.

103. TOMORROW

If there is no tomorrow
No present to rejuvenate
If there's no present
No past to ruminate
Past is the root, the foundation to make stand
The edifice of Present, the stem to withstand
Future the fruit, no one can comprehend.
Hope for the best for tomorrow, however uncertain
Time for each one bitter or sweet enters sudden
Faith is our life to enliven
May be odd or even
No problem at all
If captivate in your heart's cabin.

104. VILLAGE SIGHT AT TWILIGHT

A row of rustic ladies rushing to outskirt
With a jug of water in hands to escort
Ecstatic are cowboys behind the cattle
Returning home after a day's battle
Cattle shade awaiting the siblings in glee
Owners are agog to greet
Setting sun begules the horn to depart
Farmers hurried to leave the field apart.
Housewives ready to lit the light inside.
The candles dim in light seen outside

105. POET VS. CRITIC

Poet a man of gifted soul

Critic a man of talented soul

A poet guided by emotions and imaginations

A critic led by techniques, rules and regulations

A poet is an innate artist

A critic is a scholarly analyst

A poet is a creator of beauty

A critic is an admirer of dexterity

A poet is an inventor

A critic is a discoverer

A poet is a searcher

A critic is a researcher

106. CONQUEROR OF HEART

A scientist may invent the world of newness

A discoverer unfurls the blanket of darkness

A teacher may explore the world of knowledge

A soldier may vanquish the border of courage

But not the heart of softness the carriage to message

An emperor might conquer the vast empire

By means of money and mustle power

Leaves may fall from a bower to bower

Within a circle spreads the fragrance of a flower

But it is love that can aspire beyond despair

The whole mankind, the love inside heart can inspire

Love is love that, in no way, can conspire

An imperishable weapon to humanize

Colorless rainbow to mesmerize

Tasteless spice to naturalize

A dreamer to regain the lost paradise

Love, love, love the conqueror to universalize

Humanity at large to maximize.

107. SAVE MOTHER EARTH FROM TORTURE

What not in her lap for all living, non living beings

Soil and water beneath her heart for trees and creepers

Valleys and mountains stand still to watch civilization

Streams, rivers, rivulets rise from the core of hills

Rushes to mingle in the sea taking away one and all wills

Green forest, orchards, gardens, grassy land with cornfields

Take their shelter on the lap of mother Earth, they yield

Innumerable contributions to the world of whole mankind

Without mother Earth, nothing will exist to remind

No plants, bushes, animals, humans, insects can exist

Without caring, sharing, loving and nurturing of Earth

No demands, no expectations at all in return even dearth

She is the life of our life, soul of our life,

The nourisher, giver, and well wisher of all lives

She is the mother, nurse, anchor of human beings

She knows how to take heed of her beloved offspring's

Now on this auspicious day of worldwide celebration

Let's observe and worship the mother for her salvation

Let's do something for her to repay little of the debt

Though we cannot, still collectively strive for the best

Nothing can be done in haste,

Let's come together to stand for the care of mother not to mess

Promise, each and everybody, to keep her neat and clean

Respect her; be grateful to her kindness and forgiveness

Let's be self conscious to know her, read her, feel her helplessness
Let her grow, run, play and dream what she longs for in existence
Her highness, her goodness, her happiness can enrich
Each one with cheerfulness, love, peace, harmony that we cherish
Long live mother Earth, stay blessed and evergreen
Wishing you all the best, hope you will pardon thy children
O, humans stay away from your selfishness
To rescue mother Earth from our greediness
Save mother Earth from human torture
Nurture her to nurture mankind in juncture.

108. LANGUAGE OF PRAYER

Poetry the language of prayer directly comes from divine spirit
And enters into His heart unhurt increasing the heart beat
Without poetry of verse or free verse no prayer chanted
As without soil, air and water no seedlings planted
To haunt the abode of the Almighty, no boon granted.
Prayer well versed with music and melody tempts His mind
Heart melts away in kindness, devotee's call to rescind
Prayer in poetry doorway to the revered god or goddess
Makes one enriched with the benign grace.

109. IMPERFECTIONS

Nothing or nobody born with perfection
The Almighty is the only exception
Surrender of imperfection leads to divinity
Work with devotion can bring eternity.
Lack of comprehension, lack of loyalty
Very often the cause of failure and frailty.
Some imperfection comes closer to perfection
Through the path of patience, perseverance and rectification.
All imperfections need to be revised, remoulded, and mended
Only imperfections get a chance to be refined, reformed
Like a piece of gold sparkles forever in the end we must comprehend
Becomes the legendry instance in the annals of mankind in hand
No perfection without imperfection a naked truth to accept
As there's no rising without falling nobody can ignore the concept
Admittance of own imperfections remains above all suspect
Rightly one said, 'advice is better than precept' we have to expect.
Imperfection like childhood seeks a place, person and time
Caring, and dairing to share undoubtedly attracts like a rhyme
Suppressing imperfection like germinating seed to grow a poison tree
Before bearing the fruits better to fell the tree to be fair and free.

110. VIVID SHADES OF LOVE

Mother's touch of tender hands
Removes all filths from foot to head
Temperature of fever reduced to normal
What a magic charm in her hand
Mother's unconditional love unparallel
Makes each life a enchanted castle
Mighty power of the mundane world
Reshapes the future of children
Mother's kiss acts like a pure tonic
Nectar showers from mouth saves panic
Moulding on the anvil of ease and comfort
Never let her offspring out of effort.
Mother's humming lullaby so mesmerized
Feeds her children with oozing soothe
Naughty mind consoled to sound sleep
However the time and space dark and deep
Mother's teaching forever enriching
The goal of life even though far reaching
Each word of her sweetness so fragrant
Keeps one blessed and graced with unfaded scent.

111. MEMORIES

Memories are on tour in the chariot of time
In my mind her absence still constantly shine
Fills my heart with hightend stimulation
Drives me to the world of imagination
I don't know how it comes like a shower of rains
Some moments of my silence over me reign
A lovely word pictures painted in colors of emotions
On the slate of my heart what a wonderful creation.
Memories are past gist
Some bitter some sweet
Some forgetful some engraved
Undeleted from mind and heart.

112. DEMON OF MONOPOLY

If no reactions of any actions
And just being silent beholder then
Injustice implicitly sheltered gently
Emerges the demon of Monopoly
Regined over all mankind jovially
Randomly conquered, nothing left
Silence and ignorance vehemently
Enables one to break up at a glance
Even the iron gate of entrance
The bridge of rapport in advance.
Terrific and panic the sound of war
Bloody murderer strives to mar
Celebration of creation melts in tar
Trembled in fear, ambition goes far
Heart choked, mind blocked to debar
Sure to lead devastations no bar
Tearing heart of golden future hope
But nothing to gain or to join rope
Of peace, harmony, love, humanity,
Of justice, equality and fraternity.
War may stop beating drum
But sound continued to horn
Shedding the carpet on the head
Of the Universe, to earn ahead

Only the wages of forlorn
Being everything one sided.

113. LIFE - A. PAPER BOAT

Life swirls, twirls, whirls like a soft paper boat
Knows not on the weaving water how long floats
Water gently wets, slowly consumes little by little
Still it never loses courage to exist inspite of being brittle
Life artistic, asthetic like a dexterous paper boat
Allures the heart of the maker with its naked coat
Simply appealing, mind blowing art to teach how to live
Indisputably veritable its quandary to leave
Life is just like a paper boat floating on the water of uncertainty
How a piece of paper turns to a paper boat with dexterity
Emerged before us with the union of gail and gaiety
Truth unlocks the gate of eternity.

114. THE QUEST FOR GREATNESS

No trees bear the fruits of greatness to donate

No place is stored with piles of greatness to vacate

No market does scatter the commodities of greatness to sell

No man can purchase to garner, nobody can hail.

Nobody born with greatness on the earth

Greatness is neither health nor wealth

No particular time or season to search the greatness

Unless and until one stops chasing after selfishness

Greatness does not come to your pocket by itself

Nor is it hereditary of any race over ages to inculcate

Greatness be cultured by rendering selfless service

Without having greed, envy and malice

Dedication, sacrifice, commitment brings greatness

Positivity, righteousness, good thoughts adds sweetness.

115. WOMAN - AN INDEFINABLE CHARACTER

Man and woman two wheels of a cart

Two sides of the same coin never fall apart

But woman a character quite indefinable

Each part played by her adorable

Woman as a character unfathomable

More than deep sea, more than dense forest unreachable

Words are insufficient, inkers tired of glorifying

Poets and critics are incapable of defining

The realm of literature can't accommodate her greatness

No place remains empty to demonstrate uniqueness

Indescribable the character of women

Even dumb founded the Creator to explain

No one born to read her dashing character

Unending the story of a peerless narrator

More pages opened, more pages left to finish

Days, nights, months and years of tasks meagre to accomplish

O, woman of responsibility, equity, solidarity and versility

Let me bow my head under thy feet, goddess of magnanimity.

Wonderful, outstanding, mind-blowing, astounding nature, o womanly deity

Adjectives fade away before you, o woman thy name is beauty.

116. RED RED ROSE

Rose a flower of multi colours seen
Like moon among the stars clean
Like vermilion on women's forehead
The queen of flowers unveiled
Blooms for a purpose worthwhile
Aspires to inspire a class style
For poets similies and metaphors
For lovers a token of love and greetings
A bridge between the lover and the beloved
Connects two poles of detraction
With the power of attraction.
Ocean of fathomless tenderness
Soften the hearts of mulishness
Whose caress makes everyone sanguine?
Mirthful forgetting tons of anguish.
Symbol of victory and festiveness
Multiplies the depth of relation
Among the seekers but perishes
Within a haven of sojourn..
Eternal is its benign presence
What a magnificent creation
Can you ever sense or tense
The roses without thorns or dissipation?

117. SUMMER

THE harbinger of cooling for hearts much waiting

The bracing breeze under the mangroves invigorating

A call for jocund lovers to attend the meeting place

The scorching heat of the summer males them bold to grace

A vacation for children to enjoy playing and dancing group by group

Swimming and jumping in the river in early in the morning hails the people in troops

A vocation for the leaf gatherers to amass kendu leaf plucking one by one

Forcing them to leave behind them the sweet home alone

How mirthful village men and women to garner mahua flowers

Running to the nearby jungle with baskets on their shoulders

Amid the village veranda under the shade assembled some rustics

Busy playing cards shuffling in groups with counting sticks

Full of ecstasy full of tranquility that summer showers

Though bitter the summer sweeter are the memories left for hours?

118. UNDERSTANDING

Understanding patently makes man human
Remains not ever untouched any domain
Understanding assuredly moulds man to social
Frugal, rational, universal and above all moral
Understanding shapes human humane
Share love, care life both man and woman.
Understanding makes life so beautiful
More meaningful and more purposeful.
Understanding best weapon to vanquish
Enemies of humanity, field they relinquish
Understanding divine power to embrace
Every challenge of life with His grace.
Understanding urges establishment of worldwide peace
Prosperity, unity, equality and fraternity all eternal bliss.
Understanding solutions to all problems socio-economic and conjugal
The end of all complicated beginnings however lingering or prodigal
Understanding a talisman to conquer diverse social evils
The stones of coming with flying colours it confidently reveals.
Understanding revamps a simple home into a blest heaven
Reshaping the root of culture, habits, customs and phenomenal tradition.

119. WHY LITERACY DAY

Today International literacy Day
Internationally celebrated a red letter day
Are the illiterates really gay?
Look, what they are doing to pay
Ask them what they want to say
Illiterates are they but heart literate
Unable to read but able to read your mind
Incapable of writing but can write your heart
No trained to understand world's complexities
But they can better understand intimacy
Have you ever asked yourself who does exploit?
Literates or illiterates, educated or uneducated
Civilized or uncivilized, rustic or urban
Certainly everybody gets it
Illiterates by literates who know everything
Or literates by illiterates who know nothing
Sweet or bitter time to ponder
May be lack of letters
But not of characters
May be lack of so called understanding
But not of humane humanizing
Caring, sharing, nurturing, rupturing
Near and dear so pleasing, smiling.

120. KINDNESS

Kindness dwells inside heart and mind not in property or prosperity
A light removes darkness of hatred, fear, anger and cruelty.
Powerful eyes which can discern invisible existence of goodness
Vigilant ears that can listen the whisper of inner voices
An avid reader who can read minutely the application of requisition
A prolific writer exploring the depth beyond imagination
A sharp mind to understand the situation and character of characters
Grabs the best clues of values inside speakers and narrators.
Unending the source of kindness immortal inevitable
A little bit of kindness can change impossible to possible
Let's be kind to all standing before and behind us divine
And feel the presence of divinity we can fulfill our purpose sublime.